ELLIOTT CARTER

THREE POEMS OF ROBERT FROST

for voice and piano

Dust of Snow

The Rose Family

The Line-Gang

AMP 7454

ISBN 978-0-7935-1326-0

Associated Music Publishers, Inc.

DISTRIBUTED BY

HAL•LEONARD®
CORPORATION

7777 W. BLUEMOUND RD. P.O. BOX 13819 MILWAUKEE, WI 53213

Three Poems of Robert Frost is also available in a version orchestrated for 12 players.

Flute
Oboe
2 Clarinets
Bassoon

Guitar
Piano

Violin I
Violin II
Viola
Cello
Bass

Peformance material is available on rental from the publishers.

Dust of Snow

Robert Frost*

Elliott Carter
(1942)

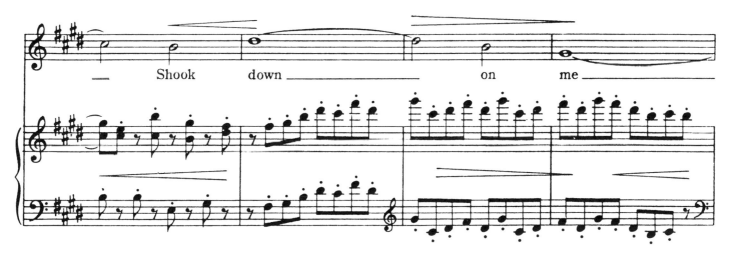

* Poem from *The Collected Poems of Robert Frost*, reprinted by permission of Henry Holt & Co.

AMP-7454

The dust _____ of snow _____

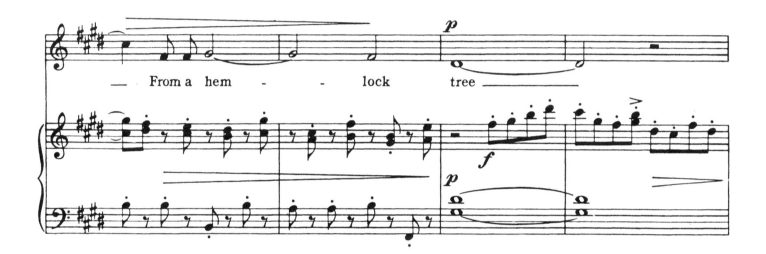

From a hem - - lock tree _____

*If performed with orchestra, there is an arpeggio here.

AMP-7454

The Rose Family

Robert Frost*

Elliott Carter
(1942)

*Poem from *The Collected Poems of Robert Frost*, reprinted by permission of Henry Holt & Co.

AMP-7454

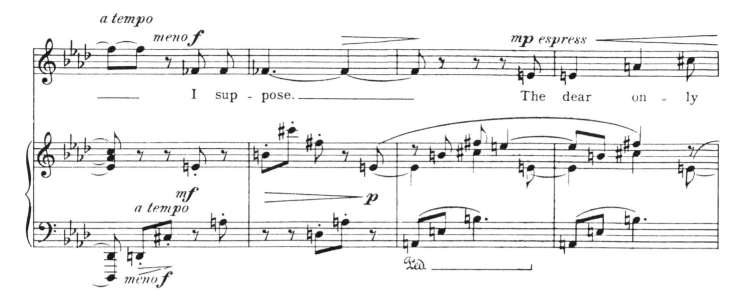

I sup - pose. The dear on - ly

knows What will next prove a rose.

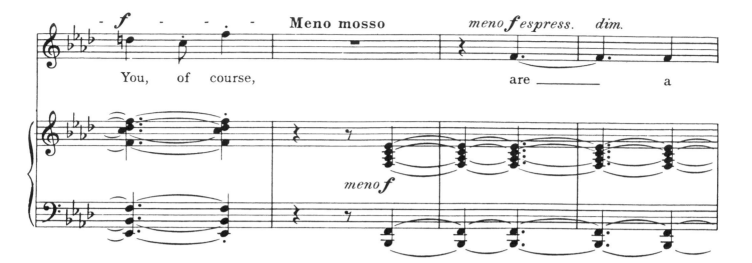

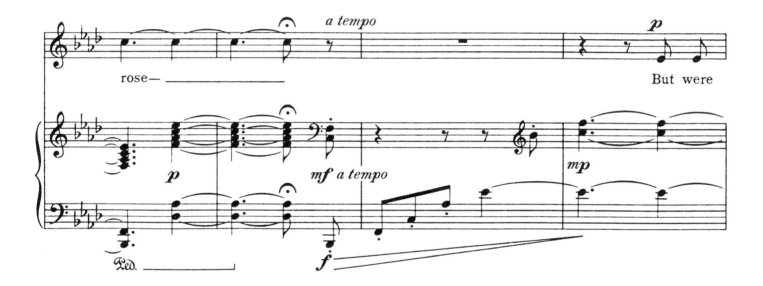

The Line-Gang

Robert Frost*

Elliott Carter
(1942)

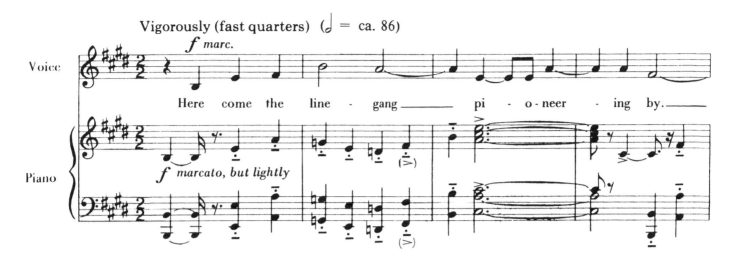

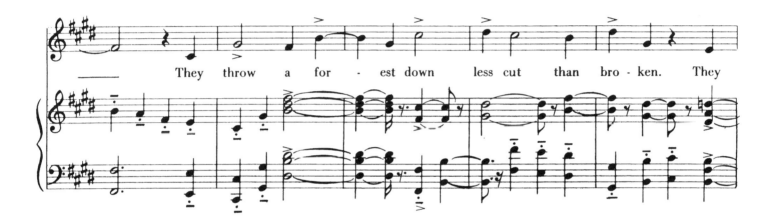

* Poem from The Collected Poems of Robert Frost, reprinted by permission of Henry Holt & Co.

AMP-7454

with a liv - ing thread.____ They string an in - stru-ment a -

gainst the sky.____ Where-in words wheth-er beat-en out or spo-ken____

will run____ as hushed as when they were a

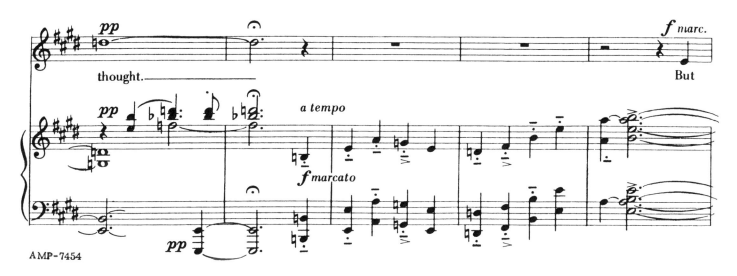

thought.____

But

in no hush _____ they string it: they go past With shouts a-

far to pull the ca-ble taut, To hold it hard _____ un-til they

slower   *a tempo*

make it fast, _____ To ease a-way they have it.

With a laugh,___ An oath___ of towns that set ___ the wild ___

___ at naught ___

They bring ___ the tel - e - phone and tel - e - graph. ___